THE ROBERTS FAMILY IN TRAVEL with KIDS

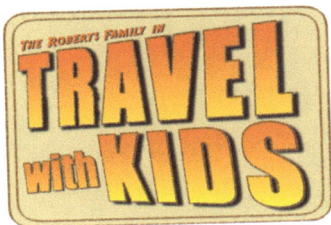

Nate & Shea's Adventures in HAWAII

By Carrie Simmons
with help and journal entries
from Nathan and Seamus,
hosts of the television series
Travel With Kids

I0087936

© 2013 Equator Creative Media In conjunction with *Travel With Kids* video series. All rights reserved. More information: TravelWithKids.tv

Aloha! That means hello in Hawaiian. Hawai'i is awesome! There are six islands that tourists can visit. Each one is really different; from the big city of Honolulu on Oahu to remote cliffs on Kaua'i to the world's most active volcano on the Big Island. There is tons to see and do: hiking, surfing, snorkeling, hula dancing and more. Join us, Nate and Shea, hosts of the television series *Travel With Kids*, as we discover a thing or two about Hawai'i's history, culture and nature and stop for lots of fun along the way!

I'm Nate!

I'm Shea!

Hawai'i is way out in the middle of the Pacific Ocean! The nearest landmass is California, over 2,000 miles away! Hawai'i has over 100 islands, but most tourists usually visit Oahu, Maui, Kaua'i, the Big Island, Moloka'i or Lana'i. Hawai'i used to be a kingdom ruled by royalty. In 1959, it became a state in the United States of America.

Did you Know...
- Hawai'i has the world's tallest sea cliffs
- Hilo, Hawai'i is the wettest city in the United States
- The world's tallest mountain is in Hawai'i*
- Kileaua is the most active volcano in the world

Kauai

Oahu · Honolulu

Molokai

Lanai   Maui

Hawai'i's flag is a combination of U.S. and British flags.

Hawaii

*When measured from sea floor

LAVA COMES THROUGH CRACK IN CRUST	COLD WATER HARDENS LAVA
HARDENED LAVA BUILDS UP	ISLAND FORMS

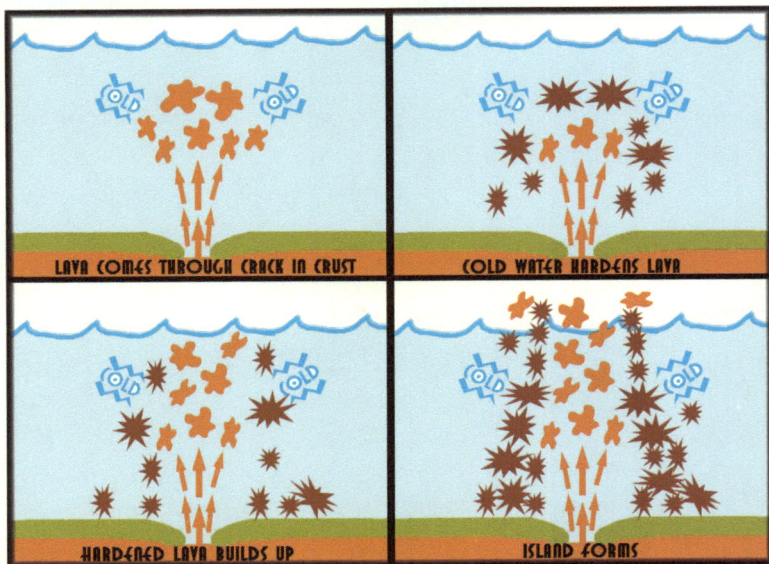

The Hawaiian Islands are old volcanoes. They formed over a hot spot. A hot spot is where lava comes through a gap in the earth's crust or seafloor. When hot lava hits cold water, it hardens to rock. The rocks pile up until they poke through the ocean's surface and presto... a new island!

Try this experiment! Ask a parent to light a candle. Pour the hot wax into cold water and see how it hardens like lava in the ocean.

3

The new island is on one of earth's tectonic plates. Each time the plate moves, a new area is over the hot spot and a new island forms. Right now a new island is forming underwater near the Big Island.

Make Your Own Volcano

Decorate with twigs.

Supplies:
- Empty yogurt container
- Modeling clay
- 1/2 cup water
- 2 tsp baking soda
- Red food coloring
- 1/2 cup vinegar
- Sand/grass/twigs

Mold clay around your container leaving a hole in the top for the lava. Add sand, grass and twigs for landscape. Pour water into container. Mix in baking soda and a couple drops of red food coloring. When you are ready for the eruption, add vinegar.

Watch the lava flow!

Volcanoes National Park

At Volcanoes National Park on the Big Island, maps show us how the islands formed. The Big Island is the newest island. Land is still being added to it everyday. Lava pours from Kilauea Volcano into the ocean and hardens making new land. It's really cool! We get to hike through hardened lava tubes, feel heat oozing out of cracks in the ground and smell sulfur...yuck! It's like rotten eggs!

Hiking in Lava Tube

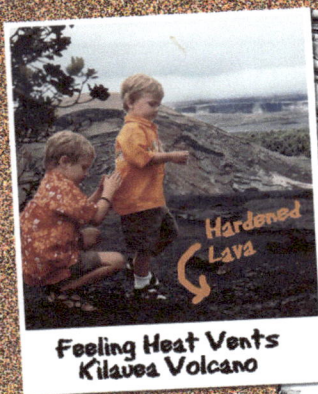

Hardened Lava

Feeling Heat Vents
Kilauea Volcano

Nate's Journal

At the volcano I felt steam from The lava coming through holes in the ground. It was so HOT!

Polynesian Migration

Hundreds of years ago, people from South Pacific islands like Tahiti and Samoa sailed outrigger canoes (canoes with pontoons on the side) to Hawai'i. They paddled across thousands of miles of open ocean using only stars and wind.

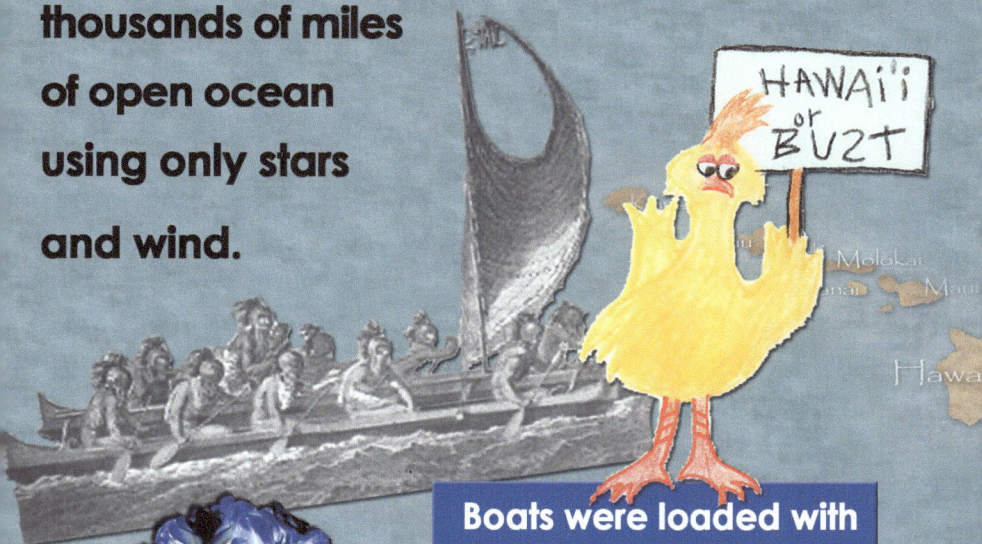

HAWAI'i or BUZT

Boats were loaded with people, plants, seeds, water and animals.

No Tools
They sailed without navigational tools like GPS or satellite.

No video games or cell phones either!

Hawaiian Gods & Goddesses

The Polynesian people brought gods and goddesses with them to Hawai'i. The myths and legends about these gods are still told today through hula dances and stories.

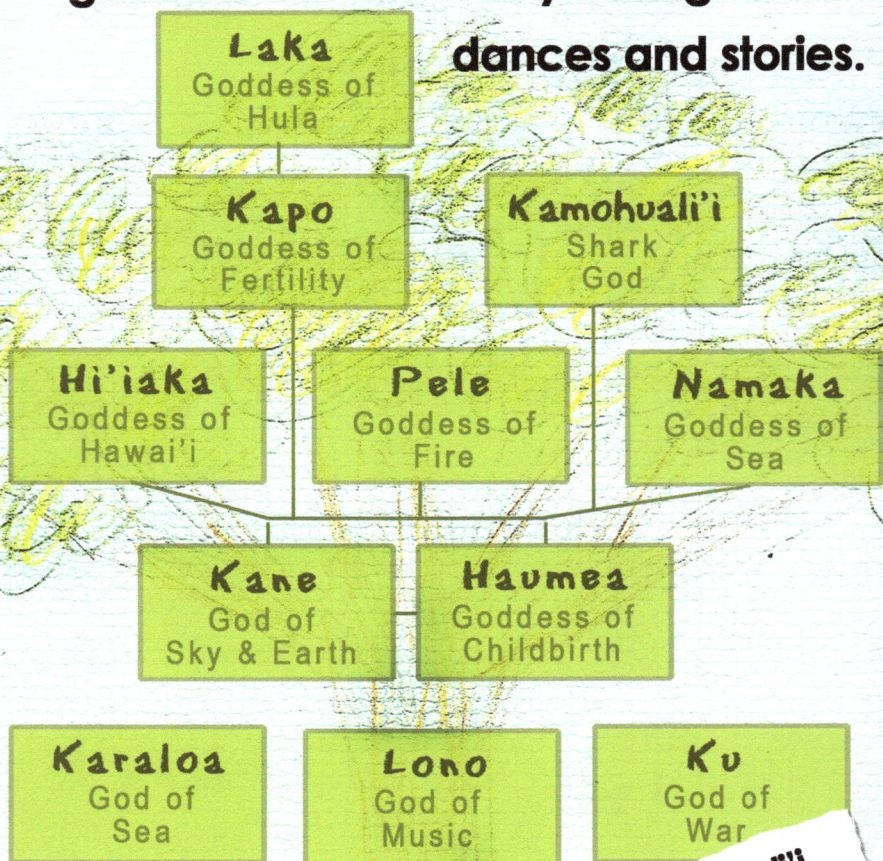

Laka
Goddess of Hula

Kapo
Goddess of Fertility

Kamohuali'i
Shark God

Hi'iaka
Goddess of Hawai'i

Pele
Goddess of Fire

Namaka
Goddess of Sea

Kane
God of Sky & Earth

Haumea
Goddess of Childbirth

Karaloa
God of Sea

Lono
God of Music

Ku
God of War

Kamohuali'i is my favorite, but I hope he's not under me when I snorkel!

The Story of Pele

Pele is the goddess of fire. Pele's father gave her a timeout from Tahiti because of her terrible temper. She was sent to sea to find a new home. Each time she landed on an island, her sea goddess sister flooded it. She finally found a home in Kilauea Volcano on the Big Island. Pele sometimes appears on deserted roads asking for food or a ride. She takes the form of a beautiful tall woman or a little old lady. Better give her what she wants because when she is mad, she turns into a flame.

Pele
by Nathan

Life in Ancient Hawai'i

In ancient Hawai'i, a person was born into a societal class and could not change it. The *ali'i* (royals) ruled the islands. People thought they had magical powers and could talk to gods. Ali'i wore capes made from bright, red feathers and tall yellow hats. They made rules called *kapu*. Punishment for breaking kapu was usually death. *Kahunas* were priests or skilled workers. *Maka'aiana* were common people who worked farms and fished. *Kauwa* were slaves captured in wars.

Coat of Arms
Royal Kingdom of Hawai'i

Nate for King! Does this hat make my head look big?

9

Hawaiian Royalty

King Kamehameha I united the islands into the Kingdom of Hawai'i. He made a law that provided safety to the elderly, women and children in war. He was one of the first world leaders to offer this type of refuge. He is known for his *Place of Refuge* on the Big Island. The last queen of Hawai'i was Lili'uokalani. In 1893, she gave up her throne under pressure from plantation owners who wanted Hawai'i to be part of the United States.

Yes...King Shea sounds much better anyway!

You can see the *Place of Refuge* at Pu'uhonua O Honaunau National Park on the Big Island. The walled-in area was a safe zone during war. It was also a safe zone for people who broke kapu. If they reached it without getting caught they were forgiven with no punishment.

Must've seen my comedy act at The Tiki Room!

Did he just call us funny?

I wish our house had a Place of Refuge!

Nate's Journal

The tikis at the Place of Refuge had funny faces carved in them. Hee Hoa

At the *Place of Refuge* and other places in Hawai'i, there are ancient fish ponds. Rock walls with gates close off part of the ocean. When fish are little they swim in and are fed lots. They get fat and can't fit back through the gates. With all the big, fat fish in the pond, it's easy to catch dinner. Many ponds were for royals only. If a *Maka'aina* fished from a royal pond, the punishment was death. Better run for the *Place* of Refuge!

We fished a lot in Hawai'i, but never in a royal pond!

Big fish, little fish... What's a *Maka'aiana* to do?

Ali'i Only!
Fish here and you'll swim with the fishes

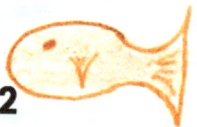

Sandwich Islands

Captain Cook must have been really hungry when he named Hawai'i. In 1778, he was the first European to see the islands. He named them The Sandwich Islands after John Montague, Earl of Sandwich in England. The next year Captain Cook landed in Kealakekua Bay on the Big Island. At first, he was treated as an honored guest, but later was killed by natives during a skirmish.

Oh look...an undiscovered island kingdom. Now, who wants a sandwich?

From Sandwich to Sugar

Captain Cook saw sugar cane when he visited Kaua'i in 1778. The first sugar cane plantation was built in 1835. Sugar was the main way Hawai'i made money. We rode the Sugar Cane Train in Maui to learn about it! People came from all over Asia to work on plantations. They brought new foods and language to Hawai'i. Bento, a Japanese box lunch, is still popular today.

Shea after too much sugar cane

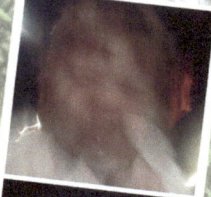

Sugar Cane Train

Nate's Journal

When they put more water in the trains steam pillows. pufft out.

14

Hawaiian Culture

Traditional culture in Hawai'i is based on Polynesian traditions brought over from South Pacific islands. Hawaiian dancing, known as hula dancing, is popular with tourists and locals. Each hula move has a meaning. Each hula dance tells a story through these moves. Use the chart on the next page to create a story.

You put your left foot in, you put your left foot out...

Hula Moves

Ocean
Roll hands forward one over the other with palms towards you

Land
Straight arms palms down. Swipe hands from one side to other.

Coconut Tree
Touch elbow to hand. Wave hand back & forth.

I or Me
Start with outstretched arms. Fold in and touch chest.

Sun
Arms in hula position. Swoop to raise above head with palms in.

Smile
Arms in hula position. Fold in to touch mouth. Pull apart & smile.

16

Polynesian Cultural Center

Fishing at PCC

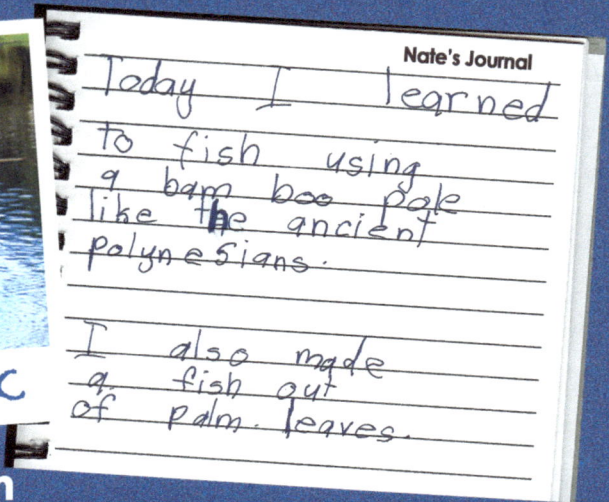

Nate's Journal

Today I learned
to fish using
a bam boo pole
like the ancient
polynesians.

I also made
a fish out
of palm leaves.

The Polynesian Cultural Center on Oahu teaches us about the people that settled in Hawai'i. There are outrigger boats like the ones they sailed here. We get to fish, taste coconut bread and make palm frond hats. We learn how to throw a spear and make faces to scare our enemies like Polynesian warriors. We even get a tattoo...temporary of course.

One cultural thing you don't want to miss in Hawai'i is surfing. Riding the waves has been a part of Hawai'i's history for a long time. European explorers back in James Cook's day said they saw Hawaiians surf. Ali'i strutted their stuff on the waves to show off their power.

Hang Ten Dude!
Ride with all ten toes hanging over the front of your board

Surfing

Surf Speak:
Natural Foot: Left-foot forward
Goofy Foot: Right-foot forward
Getting Barreled: Riding in the tube of a wave
Dude/Brah: Friend
Grommet: Surfer Kid
Carve: Turn hard

Nate's Journal

Surfing feels like flying on the waves

Other than English, and a few Asian languages, there are two main languages spoken by locals - traditional Hawaiian and Hawai'i Creole English also known as Pidgin. Check out the phrases on the next page to make your own sentences.

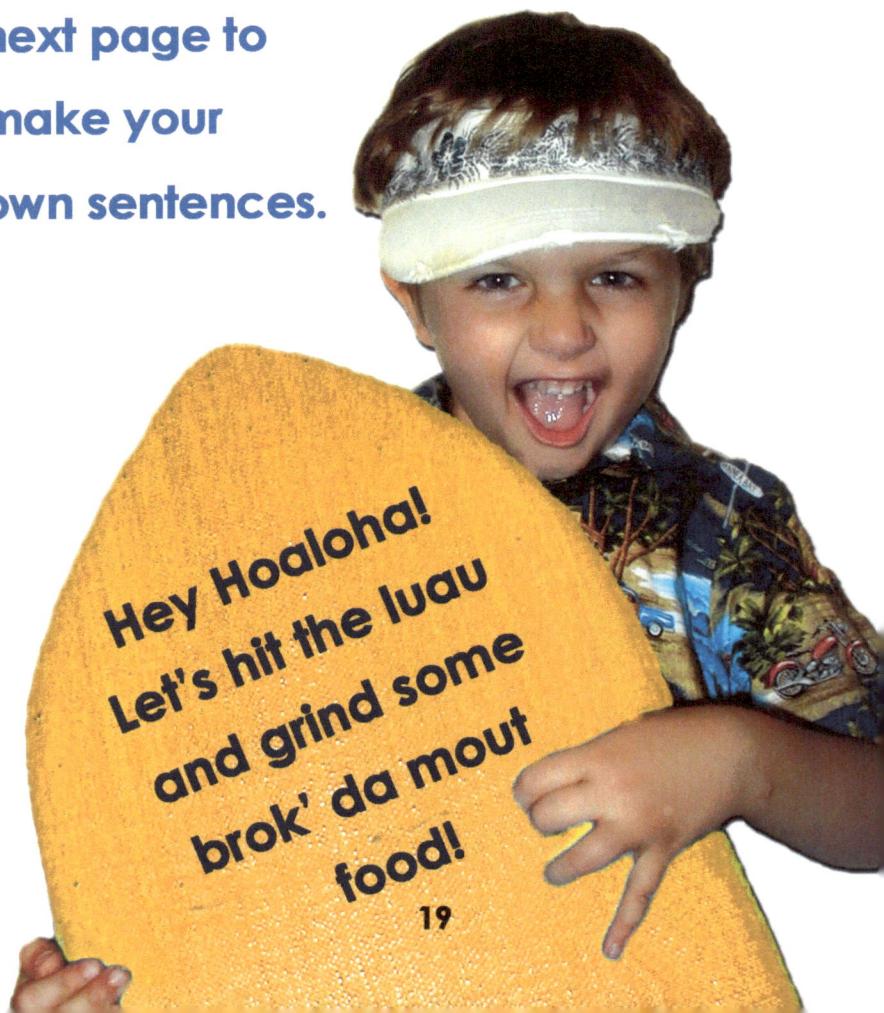

Hey Hoaloha! Let's hit the luau and grind some brok' da mout food!

19

English	Hawaiian	Pronunciation
Hello/Bye	Aloha	Ah-loh-ha
Please	Hó 'olu	Hoh-oh-loo
Thank you	Mahalo	Mah-ha-loh
Yes	'Ae	I
No	'A 'ole	Ah-oh-lay
Child	Keiki	Keh-ee-kee
Friend	Hoaloha	Hoh-ah-loh-hah
Feast	Lu'au	Loo-ow
Party	Ho' olaule'a	Hoh-oh-low-lay-ah
Cheers!	Hipahipa!	Heepah-Heepah
Delicious	'Ono	Oh-no
Surf	He e nalu	Hay eh nah-loo
Turtle	Honu	Hoh-noo
Whale	Kohola	Koh-hoh-lah
Dolphin	Nai'a	Nah-ee-ah
Shark	Mano	Mah-no

Pidgin

Grind	Eat until you're stuffed.
Bumbye	Later on, after awhile
Bummahs	Bummer/disappointed
Brok' da mout	Delicious
Akamai	Smart
Kay den	OK

Now hear this:

Humuhumuunu-kunukuapua'a

It's one of the longest words in the world. It means trigger fish in Hawaiian.

Hawaiian Food

Hawai'i's food reflects its role as a tropical paradise with lots of sweet flavors! One not-so-sweet flavor that takes getting used to is poi. Poi is a traditional Hawaiian dish made from the taro root. It's like the mashed potatoes of Hawai'i, but it's purplish-grey. A great way to get a taste of Hawaiian food is at a luau. It's a huge feast with hula dancing.

Don't eat me! In the early 1700s dog was on the menu, but not anymore!

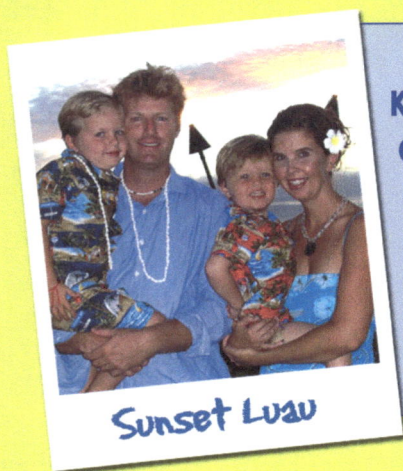

Sunset Luau

Luau Menu

Kalua Pig - Pig cooked underground
Chicken Laulau - Wrapped in ti leaves
Poi - Mashed taro root
Poke - Raw Fish
Lomi Lomi Salmon - More Raw Fish
Haupia - Coconut Pudding
Don't worry they usually have a "Kid's Menu" too!

Macadamia Crusted Mahi Mahi

- 4 Mahi-Mahi fillets
- 1/2 cup flour
- 1/4 cup macadamia nuts, crushed
- 1/2 cup butter, melted
- 8 strips of bacon
- Shredded coconut (optional)

Heat oven to 350 degrees. Combine flour and nuts. Coat fillets with butter. Dip into flour mixture. Wrap with bacon. Cook 15 minutes. Raise temperature to 400 degrees. Top with shredded coconut if desired. Cook an additional 5 minutes. Serve with fresh mango.

On the fruitier side of things, Hawai'i rocks! Here are some of the fruits we tried:

Pineapple - Hawai'i's famous for them. They're prickly and yellow and grow on the ground.

Coconut - Coconuts grow in the trees Keep your eyes up and wear a hard hat!

Guava - These small red or yellow fruits smell like roses and taste sweet.

Mango - Oval shaped green and red fruit that smells like perfume, but tastes sweet.

DANGER
FALLING FRUIT

LOVE a GUAVA

Guava Farm, Kaua'i

Hawaiian Plants & Flowers

Hawai'i is a lush place filled with amazing plants and flowers. Because it's located so far from land, many species of plants here, only grow here! The plumeria tree has flowers like the white ones on this page They smell sweet. The hibiscus is the state flower. The Kukui nut, or Candlenut, tree is the state tree.

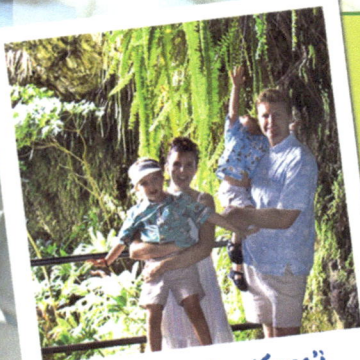

Fern Grotto, Kaua'i

The Fern Grotto in Kaua'i has trails passing tropical flowers and fruit trees. A big hurricane tore most of the ferns down. So, they used a dart gun to shoot new seedlings back onto the cliffs and caves.

One cool thing Hawaiians do with flowers is make leis. They string flowers together to make a necklace or a headband.

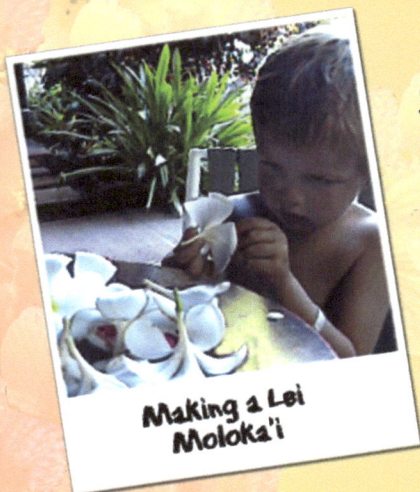

Making a Lei
Moloka'i

Make A Lei

Supplies:
- Flowers (gather some from the ground at your hotel in Hawai'i or at home)
- Heavy Thread (cut long enough to slip over head)
- Kid-Safe Needle

Thread needle. Knot the end of the thread. Push center of flower over needle and down to the end of the thread. Continue until thread is full. Knot and tie ends together. Place around recipient's neck saying "Aloha" with a kiss on the cheek.

Hawaiian Animals

Hawai'i has lots of unique animals! Many of the birds here are only found in Hawai'i. Life under the waves is very colorful. In winter you can see humpback whales. Check out the Hawaiian names for these animals!

Roosters were brought over on boats from Tahiti. During 1992 Hurricane Iniki, high winds blew open cages and Kaua'i's roosters flew the coop and still roam free today.

I'm out of here!

Honeycreeper
I'iwi

Hawaiian Goose
Nene

I saw a honu near Ke'e Beach in Kaua'i

Dolphins are
really playful
and fun
I got
to hug them
and do tricks.

Swimming with Dolphins
Big Island

Turtle

Honu

Humpback Whale
Na Kohola

Dolphin
Nai'a

Shark
Mano

Ilio holo I Kauaua
Monk Seal

26

Now that you know a little bit about Hawai'i's history and culture, it's time to go check it out for yourself. We've made a list of our favorite things to do on each island. Whether you try them at home (think...surfing in the bathtub or try some of the crafts in this book) or actually go for a visit, have fun getting into the Aloha Spirit! To continue your Hawaiian vacation, check out the video series, *Travel With Kids Hawaii.*

Best beginner surf spots:
- Waikiki, Oahu
- Po'ipu, Kaua'i
- Lahaina, Maui

Oahu

Polynesian Cultural Center

Snorkeling, Shark's Cove

Chinatown, Honolulu

Pearl Harbor

Stingray Pool, SeaLife Park

Must-Do Oahu

- ☐ Surf Waikiki Beach
- ☐ Eat in Chinatown
- ☐ Snorkel Shark's Cove
- ☐ Learn about WWII at Pearl Harbor
- ☐ Soak in the culture at the Polynesian Cultural Center
- ☐ Snorkel with stingrays at SeaLife Park
- ☐ Eat from a shrimp truck on North Shore

Kaua'i

Na Pali Coast

Po'ipu Beach

Fishing on Kaua'i

Hanapepe Swing Bridge

Must-Do Kaua'i

☐ Play in the waves on Po'ipu Beach

☐ Fish in Koke'e State Park in Waimea Canyon

☐ Spot turtles while snorkeling near Ke'e Beach

☐ Cross swinging bridge & eat shave ice in Hanapepe

☐ Hike Kalalau Trail to Hanakapi'ai Falls, Na Pali Coast

☐ Drive along North Shore past Hanalei

Maui

Road to Hana

Banyan Tree, Lahaina

Luau on Ka'anapali

Sunset at Black Rock

Must-Do Maui

- ☐ Have a picnic along the Road to Hana
- ☐ Hang out under the Banyan Tree in Lahaina
- ☐ Check out the cliff divers at Black Rock
- ☐ Attend a sunset luau
- ☐ Build a sandcastle on Ka'anapali Beach
- ☐ Take a snorkel cruise

Lava Tube, Kilauea

Place of Refuge

Parker Ranch

Dolphin Swim

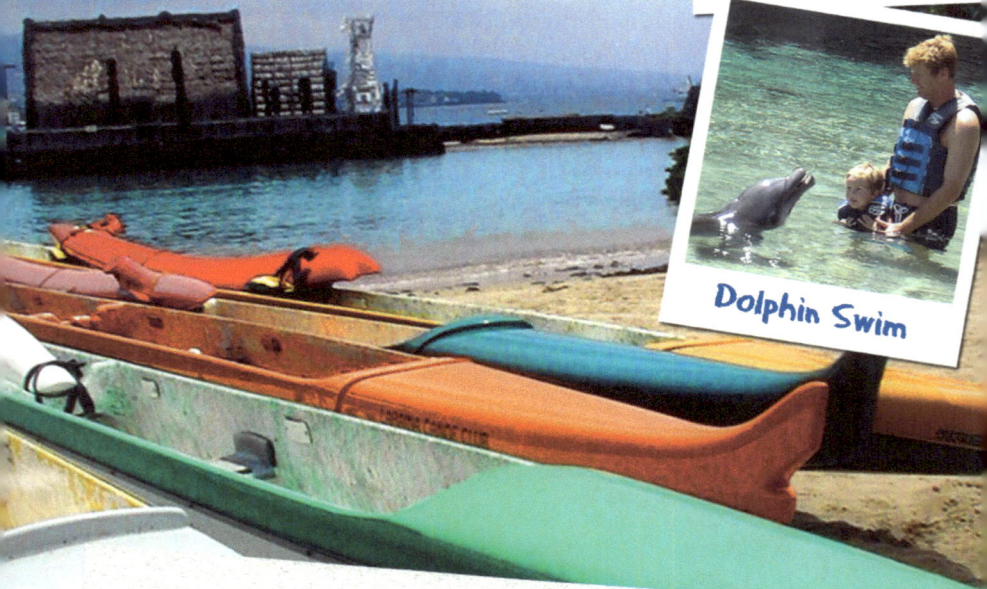

Must-Do Big Island

- ☐ Hunt for lava at Volcanoes National Park
- ☐ Meet tikis at Pu'uhonua O Honaunau National Park
- ☐ Climb the world's tallest mountain
- ☐ Swim with dolphins at Waikaloa Village
- ☐ Ride horses at Parker Ranch
- ☐ Eat a malasada

Moloka'i & Lana'i

Snorkeling, Lanai

Post-A-Nut

Fr. Damien Church

Beachcombing

Must-Do Lana'i

- [ ] Snorkel in Hulopo'e Bay
- [ ] Look for treasures on Shipwreck Beach
- [ ] Hike Koloiki Ridge Trail for amazing views

Must-Do Moloka'i

- [ ] Ride mule to Kalaupapa Peninsula to learn about Fr. Damien.
- [ ] Hike to waterfall in Halawa Valley
- [ ] Send a coconut postcard

32

Nate & Shea's Adventures provides information about destinations around the world. Learn history, culture and nature by taking a virtual trip with your guides Nate and Shea.*Nate & Shea's Adventures* can be used as a companion guide to the *Travel With Kids* video series or on their own.

Look for these other *Travel With Kids* products:

Nate & Shea's Adventures in:
Hawaii, South Africa, New York, Alaska Peru, London, Ireland, Wales, Italy, Florida

Travel With Kids (DVD):

United States:
Alaska
Florida
Hawaii: Oahu
Hawaii: Kaua'i
Hawaii: Maui & Moloka'i
Hawaii: Big Island
New York
San Diego

Caribbean:
Bahamas
Caribbean Cruise
Jamaica
Puerto Rico & Virgin Islands

Europe:
England
Greece
Ireland
Italy
London
Paris
Scotland
Wales

Latin America:
Costa Rica
Mexico: Yucatan
Mexico: Baja
Peru

Episodes covering additional destinations available on Hulu, iTunes, Amazon and more

Find out more at TravelWithKids.tv!

www.ingramcontent.com/pod-product-compliance
Lightning Source LLC
Chambersburg PA
CBHW040346060426
42445CB00029B/19